Thoughts in Vision

Poetic Works of Love, Life and Inspiration

For:

_____

From:

_____

Thoughts in Vision

Poetic Works of Love, Life
and Inspiration

E. Arabis Zemill

Thoughts in Vision

Manufactured in the United States of America.

For information about the publisher, please contact:
The P3 Press
16200 North Dallas Parkway, Suite 170
Dallas, Texas 75248

www.thep3press.com
(972) 248-9500

A New Era in Publishing™

ISBN-13: 978-1-933651-85-9
ISBN-10: 1-933651-85-7
LCCN: 2010911649

For information about the author, please contact:
Lyrics Unlimited
www.AttentionRequired.com
(877) 359.9779

Author contact information:
www.EArabisZemill.com
info@EArabisZemill.com

This Book Is Dedicated To:
My Mother Shirley
And
My Brother Yul

All My Love

Table of Contents

Preface

From the moment the concept of placing some of my thoughts into a more formal format appeared in my mind, the blueprint for this purpose had already been written. That purpose was to share these words in hopes that others would appreciate the thoughts, share with someone, lift a troubled spirit, and inspire a hungry mind. It started with the acknowledgment of a divine gift of word and expression and then traveled from the genesis of thought to the reality of existence.

In my heart I felt there were things that I had written that were insightful and moving. I remember times when I had friends back in the day who couldn't express themselves as easily as I could, who would ask me to write something for someone they cared about. I had all these things locked inside, and writing was a way to release those feelings. Those creative people out there, as they read these pages, will recognize that sometimes you have things in your head that are so powerful that you can't sleep until you write them down or put them on tape. I have to keep a recorder within arm's length at all times. It's crazy, but it's true.

There were words that were spoken that had meaning and told an inspired story. There were lines on the pages of my text that were thought provoking. There was truth in what I expressed. Not from a place of ego or being full of myself did I feel these things about what I had written, but from a place of humility and knowing the source of the inspiration. There are millions of gifted people in the world, but there are few who truly pursue their passion as a means of supporting their lives.

My motivation to go forward with this book was in part due to the fact that, after working in corporate America for over twenty years, I realized that I had always been on someone else's payroll. I work for a great company that has provided a good life, but there was still something missing. It was like that proverbial "pebble in my shoe." I said to myself, "I've been writing poetry and songs all my life but never did a thing with my work." There were those that always said I should get out and throw my name in the hat with others who were doing the same thing. I know life has no guarantees and that talent alone does not claim success. I told myself that if I did this with honesty of purpose, drive, and persistence, anything was possible. And if there were only twenty people in the whole world that thought enough of me to acquire my work, at least I can say I finished what I started. I'd thank them for their generosity. It would be a dream fulfilled. We should always set goals, make plans, and diligently pursue our dreams. Always work to finish what you start.

Then there was the fear of job cuts—losing everything that I had worked so hard to achieve. Coming from the projects, getting a degree, having a nice home; all of it could end with a pink piece of paper. At that moment, I really had to take inventory of what I had done and what my legacy might be. I thought that many of the things I had written were poems that may be relevant to others. It was more than just rhyme and meter. It was real-life situations, real thoughts, real feelings, and images expressed in poetic form. Again, it was a dream that became a goal. A plan was then formulated. You have to put your vision into motion. "Then," I said, "what if I go completely off the radar and add quotes that I've made throughout my life that came from me, by way of my inspired experiences. Each poem would have a message that led you into each poem. I've read many poetry books and have never seen that. It would be a setting of the stage for what you are about to read."

The poems would come from my walk of life. I've known love in a very passionate way. I've felt the pain of the loss of my mother and brother. I made it out of a concrete jungle. I've had to deal with prejudice face-to-face. I've had relationships where I could really appreciate the love of a good woman and the drama of ones that I should have passed by. I know the value of real friends and a close family.

I did not set out to write about all these things; this is just the way the pen flowed. I feel that everyone who reads this body of work will find something they can relate to. For the men out there who stumble, trying to find the right words to say, feel free to pull something from these pages. Just try not to tell her too many times it came from you because she might have the book. I'm just teasing. For the women who honor me with your presence, there are words written totally with you in mind. To the young men and young women, we need you to raise the bar and become all you were meant to be.

I understand that too often we take for granted this moment in the continuum of time to unimaginable heights. I see nature and all that surrounds us as a mural we did not create. I understand the wonderment of a peaceful spirit and having favor. I am a strong man who stands tall in the face of adversity. I love life and have lived it. Experiences are meant to be shared; these poems are a collection presented as a vehicle of my expressions.

—E. Arabis Zemill

Acknowledgments

Each of us was born with a gift that is unique to the individual but universal in scope. I believe it is our responsibility to take our gift and let it be the driving force in all that we passionately pursue. I am thankful and blessed that the Creator has shown me favor, and because of His favor, I am able to share this book with you.

To Cynthia and Jenni, who believed this project was relevant and said it was a collection of beautiful and well-written pieces: you helped inspire me to go forward with this book.

To Cynthia, who worked to guide me through this maze of presentation: thank you for your time and enthusiasm.

To Jenni, who, I was informed, was my toughest critic: you lit a fire that said I could do this, and you showed love for the art of my words.

To Marion, who showed tireless dedication and support, made the phone calls, the connections, and typed the pages: you helped make this happen.

To my brother, Byron, who has kept the faith and is fighting the good fight, his wife Karla, and all the kids: thank you for your love.

To Jonathan, Trina, and Ombrey: keep your eyes on the prize.

To Tamara Edwards of TEGA Creative Studio: your graphic designs are off the charts.

To photographer Kauwuane Burton: thanks for your great eye behind the camera.

To Monica and Todd of Epitome Magazine: thank you for believing in me enough to publish my first piece of work. Much love and success to you both.

To Mike, Dennis, and Bobby, my road dogs: keep it pushing.

To the Pope family, the Hall family, and Betty and Jessie Staton: thank you for your love and support.

To Eric Dickerson, hall of famer, and Charles Drayton, my college teammates: you both always said I had it; I just needed to do something with it. Thank you.

To all my close friends and family: I thank each and every one of you for your love and support.

To all the readers, the fans, the book clubs, and the people who support this project: a sincere thank you.

I

Shades of Love

My Process of Thoughts

*L*ove is arguably the most pronounced of all the things that touch our hearts. It comes in many colors, levels of depth and expressions. The words that follow are an attempt to view love in all its vastness and the feelings it evokes. To examine its beauty, power, the pain and benevolence. I believe too often we take love for granted. Moreover, do we even know what real love is? One of the most prevalent flaws in the dynamics of love is our inability to communicate what we are feeling. Openness, honesty and trust are not just words to fill in the blanks of a strained conversation. They are the building blocks that are the foundation of a lasting relationship. From a very real perspective, let us now explore the many *Shades Of Love.*

The genesis of love
Is spiritual in its origin

What is love?

Love Is

Love is
A rush of elation that cannot be contained
Love is
A whisper that resonates as calamity
Yet still craved again and again.
Love is
A yearning that amplifies a beating heart
It is the beginning and awakening of a connecting start.
Love is
A gamble that we all play in hopes to win
It reaches as deep as the roots of a sequoia tree,
That seamlessly never ends.
Love is
A wonder, a gentle stroke, as light as a leaf on the wind,
It is the alpha and omega, the beginning
And the end.
True love is,

Divine.

The story of our love, was wrtten
by residence of heaven.

An Affair Of The Stars

*Y*ou are the highlight of my millennium. It is no
mystery that our intimacy consists of fragments of
unnamed worlds. From the moment you crystallized in my
view, there was no doubt we would become the
caretakers of the other's heart. I submit, the galaxy has
summoned me for you intently. You responded,
"There shall be for me, no other." Here in this station of
creation, lies unparalleled admission
of aligned devotion.

*Real is the fantasy whose destination
is enlightenment.*

Come With Me

I know you've been hurt so many times before,
Lied to so often until you said your heart you'll give no more.
I'm here to show you a better way,
To take you to a place where there's no end of day.

Where water falls will embrace you and sunlight
endlessly shines through.
There's a scent of jasmine that mingles in the breeze,
It compels anything in thought, to luminous deeds.

We will lay on the banks of white-like sands,
Cover ourselves in sunflower petals,
Across our hearts the allure of laughter we will brand.

The sounds of night, to us they will listen,
To the love we make as the moonlight glistens.
Take my hand and come with me,
To a place called "you and I,"
That few will ever see.

It is the little things that
Engage a woman's heart.

For You

*H*ere is a flower I chose for you. In the garden of the
Widow Elliott do I confess I entered uninvited.
More colorful than a rose and unknown to me its formal
name, I removed it from its home of cheerful décor.
But as I passed her labored soil, I could not help but bask
in the beauty of its radiance. From my pantry I found this
vase, that used to grace the window of my aunt long past.
With care did I run the water where its stem now rests
with nourishment. The pastel petals open to your
presence, bringing fragrance to your allure.

Patience in love will preserve a golden heart.

Love Takes Time

You cannot rush a masterpiece, this you will see
For many a millennium has it waited, it has waited to be.
To touch the very core of your soul,
Its journey is the sum of endless waters,
And stories yet untold.
As the tides roll through distant lands.
It leaves behind the power of might,
With an echo of demand.

Wait for the moment, wait to know it's right,
And when in splendor it appears to your heart,
it will give a radiant light.
It is enduring, it is pain,
If you ever possessed it,
Held it close to your breast and lost it,
You will never be the same.

Take your time to truly understand, you must be sure,
For love loves nobody, it exists in the outer atmosphere,
It carries no sign of acknowledgement,
When it's broken, only time is its cure.

But when it is genuine, a marvel it is to behold,
More precious than all the world's
wonders, and yes even gold.
So be patient, let it come by its own railway line,
For if it is yours to have and theirs to give,
It lasts beyond the infinity of time.

If you choose to leave
The time has come to go.

Moving On

*A*t love's last glance have I cried out,
Knowing the end has come and there is no doubt.
For all the years that have traced our path,
The image of soliloquy could no longer make it last.

Maybe it was you, maybe it was me,
We both found our love lost of destiny.
With a heavy heart I must turn away,
For the sunlight in my eyes consumes me,
on a dark and empty day.

Sometimes you have to let it go,
Sometimes you just have to do the best you can,
Sometimes we play with peoples' hearts,
Like children who build castles in the sand.

Be not afraid or dismayed,
it is simply a time that has come to be,
Life has made a different path,
For both you and me.
When the candle goes dim and its
glow is withered and gone,
Nothing left for past lovers of lust
but to then, move on.

A broken heart can never mend,
Until the wall built around it will
allow light to come in.

The Last Time I Knew Love

You ask me if I loved you,
You said tell you, if I really do,
But my heart gave way to silence,
Along came my lips, as they did too.

I'm sorry for not giving you the words,
The words I know you want to hear,
I can only tell you I care,
And how much I enjoy having you near.

It's been a long time since I felt,
The emotions that you do,
The winds of time have crossed many decades,
Since I've harbored a nuance so true.

I remember the day, I remember the hour,
When the image of real love then lost its power.
It was the day I laid my heart on a table,
And gave it willingly when you didn't even have to ask,
Sent away down a broken road, you shattered it,
Was when I knew love last.

Remember the things that are important to her,
And peace will dwell in your household.

Don't Miss Her Day

I don't care what you do or what you say,
Don't miss her birth or Valentine's Day.
With hell you know you will have to pay,
If a candy, a card or flowers don't come her way.

Men you don't know, you just don't understand,
If you are the one in her life, you better do the best you can.
Now if she's single and there is no one around,
She'll get over seeing deliveries, not for her desk
are they bound.

But if she has somebody, and again you are the man,
Let me say you better do, do the very best you can.
Other holidays are special, she loves them too,
But on these two days you better come through.

I'm telling you what I know and not what I've heard,
To fellas everywhere, I'm trying to spread the word.
Make it to that store or florist before they close,
Or when you get home, expect rolling eyes and a
turned up nose.

So for the last time, hear me when I say,
Don't forget her birth or Valentine's Day.
Please don't end up like me; I had to rent a room,
Her Birthday was Valentine, they both came too soon.

The curious gaze of a stranger
Is often an alluring invitation.

Warm Eyes

*F*rom across the room you call me.
The glare of your stare tells me I'm too far away,
You want me nearer.
Highlighting the twinkle of your invitation
Is the gaze from me that says I hear you.
A closer examination of the anticipation escalates.
The fire that burns so brightly draws me closer.
My senses respond to the fragrance of your indulgence.
I'm here, I see the mystery in those brown hypnotics.
As the moment insisted, your warm eyes persisted,
It is now time to know who you are.

Warm thoughts ignited cherished memories.

Touched

And she wrote to me,

I smile, when I hear your thoughts in my head.

Don't let something you didn't say,
Be the reason you walked away.

Talk To Me

I wish I was able to read your thoughts,
I would then not have to steal them, they could be bought.
For a penny or a dime, I would know in time,
The words you will not say, locked in your mind.

We used to talk all night, to every end of the day.
Now few words are spoken, it seems very little to say.
How can I help you, how can you not see,
If you don't open up, there could be no you or me.

We have to talk face-to-face,
Not with a text or some email,
We have to get back to a time,
When what we're feeling could be seen,
the eyes would always tell.

Share with me the problem, whatever it is, good or bad,
I will listen to your expressions, release will make me glad.
Tell me what's going on, I promise my trust is in you,
Have not the years we've shared meant something,
Have I not always come through?

We have to talk to each other,
And not let a day go by,
To give all we have to give,
To keep this love alive.

So here at this moment come and take my hand,
Together we will seek answers, together I know we can.
This is our time to remember, our time to make a stand,
We vowed to face anything together,
Because you're my lady and I'm your man.

The face tells the story
That the lips fail to confess.

I'm Sorry

*T*here are no words that can soothe
this flawed indiscretion.
My hope is simply that the resolution,
Does not go beyond the compass of your forgiveness.
Punish me with your silence,
But offer me then a doorway to atonement,
And take not from me,
The pleasure of your company.

Show in deeds your intentions
And I will say in words my affirmations.

Do You Have To Ask?

*W*hat do I have to do to prove my love?
Each day I hold you it's in my touch,
The moment I kiss you it's in my lips.
The gifts I give, come from the heart,
The doors I open, the chairs I pull, before dinners start.
The smile of your reflection that covers me,
The morning kiss, the long hug good-bye,
With each breath I breathe I feel you,
Your passion makes me high.
The blood that flows through my soul,
Will warm you in the night and long winter's cold.
My heart is my present to you,
Can't you see, my love is shown in everything I do.
There is a part of you that will always exist in me,
And when I'm near you, even those without sight can see.
With every fiber of my being,
I know,
You are woven in the very fabric of my heart.
If I am the fire,
You are the spark.

Healing can only begin
When refusal of that acceptance ends.

Why

*W*hat do you mean I can't go away?
Who are you not to let me say 'bye?
You said you didn't want me anymore,
So why in the hell do I need to try?

How do you know it's over?
What can you show that gives me proof,
When all the time we've been together,
You never once told the truth.

Maybe you're right, it's time to just walk away,
It's hard trying to talk to someone, who has nothing to say.
I wonder if you ever loved me, did you even care?
Don't bother answering the question, everything shows,
you were never there.

So now the time has come, when we
must truly say good-bye,
No need to ask any questions, no need to wonder why.
Sometimes it's just best to walk away,
just let it go when you're through,
When you can't even answer why,
There's nothing left to do.

A love worth holding on to
Is worth going through the fire to keep.

Never Give Up On Love

*H*ello darling, thought I'd call to take a few minutes
To let you know what I was really feeling.
You know as I look back on all the things we've shared,
On all the love we've made, one thing comes to mind
That I simply can't seem to forget,

And that's that you have always been a very special part of me
And I long to be and hope that I'm always that part of you.
As we travel through life's vast horizons,
Go through the highs and lows of love,
I hope to find new dreams, new aspirations, new destinies
All of which I want to share with you.

You know sometimes there will be differences
There will be ups and there will be downs
And there will be moments when you and I
Won't see eye-to-eye on all the things we care to seek
But as long as we continue to love
As long as we continue to share
As long as we continue to communicate,
The things we feel in our hearts will not waiver
And there's nothing that can stand in the way of our love.

You'll always be a part of me,
and that part of me which exists in you
I believe will live eternally.
And when I wake up in the morning, open my eyes,
roll over and see you there, it makes me smile,
Because I know you've shared all of that with me.

So when the day ends and our love begins
I reach out my arms and hold my hands open to you
And hoping that you share the feeling that I do too.
I guess what I'm trying to tell you
Is how much that I love you.
And sometimes the words seem meaningless
They seem trivial and don't seem to amount to say
All the things I really want to say and feel.

I don't really know if you can place them into words
I don't know if you can put them in a way
That would express what's going on deep inside my heart.
But when I think of you it makes me want to sing
It makes me want to write melodies of love,
of happiness, of joy and peace
Because you are so beautiful you mean so much
I'm never gonna give up on love
I'm never gonna give up on us
Hold these thoughts true to you
And all that we share

Whenever you're feeling down
Or whenever you're feeling blue,
Think of us, think of me, think of you.

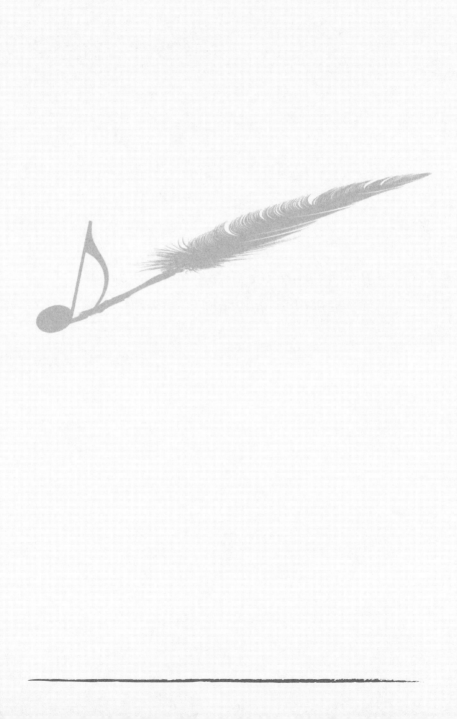

Precious are the simple moments that become enduring memories.

A Memory In The Flame

*A*s we lay beneath this padded quilt,
Watching the flicker of the fires glow,
I'm reminded of the moment we met,
On a slope of white powder,
In the arms of winter's snow.

I remembered then, as I do now,
What you whispered in my ear,
Ours is a love eternal,
It is the warmth of my heart,
Which you hold so dear.

When the moment is right it
will last beyond the night.

Last Night

*G*entle is the caress of a warm and caring hand,
Softly are the words that reach,
Where no thoughts had place to land.
New is the feeling, I've longed to come to know,
Triggered by the way you loved me last night,
And how I've longed for you so.

I wish I could take that pleasure,
And preserve it just for me,
And whenever I was feeling alone,
Like a Genie I would rub that bottle,
And instantly you I would see.

Last night was more than the first time,
More than the first time for us,
We both knew it was a moment of magic,
Two hearts were given an eternal rush.

Sensual senses cannot be contained, only expressed.

Lust

I lay awake at night with the thought of you pounding my head like a hammer to a nail. My blood boils as visions of you dance on the table of my imagination. My palm sweats as I await your arrival. My body burns in the nectar of your delight. Each stroke you take is an eternity across my soul. My eyes glance at the amazement of your sultriness. My arms beckon your body as the moment of your sensation greets me with elation. Locked in a fierce embrace we cling to one another as a vine to a towered tree. With each breath I breathe you; inhale my satisfaction from the clinging of our thrusts. No words are spoken yet volumes of our intense encounter resonate through these hollow walls. We are obsessed. We indulge our seduction without reservation and without restrictions. Without the knowledge of the other's name.

There is assurance in listening.

I'm Here

*J*ust say the words and I will listen,
There can be no us, if trust is missing.
Speak without thought and know that I will hear,
Believe that I will bring calm,
To whatever you may fear.

So simple these three words
So lasting their mark on your heart.

I Love You

I love you and I believe in my
heart I always will.
Though time may pass,
And seasons endlessly change,
I will love you,
Still.

Passion performed leaves behind
traces of lasting desire.

Letter To My Lover

*A*s I lay here satiated in bed before I fall asleep,
the sweetness of your scent caresses my
senses softly as they move across my face,
As if your hands were there to trace the lines of my smile.

I rolled over to find the place you laid,
Holds the nectar of your splendor,
And yields echoes of the delight of our pleasured excursion.
I caress the pillow that made home your rest,
I see your smile in the grooves of the movement
of my sheets.

I awake to find that dawn is now
upon me and a new day arises.
The sunlight summons my inclinations,
And from miles away your voice calls to me, it says . . .

Hear me, the thoughts of last evening boil in my blood,
My entrance is still moist from your explosion.
The walls of my sensual cave throb soft and warm,
I await your return. The moments in the hour,
Pass even now so soon, yet chains me to anticipation.
Again do I call out to you, my love,
Oh how I miss you.

The beauty within
Can only be seen with sincere eyes.

You Are

I love you not because of your hair or your eyes,
It is the beauty I see, when I look inside.
Oh I smile, I know when I sleep,
Because dreams of you are all I keep.

Tell me that you love me,
Tell me my love, give me a clue,
Does your heart sputter as does mine,
With visions of mercurial images of me and you?

Oh, you are beautiful,
An angel for the world to see,
On a glittering star falling from heaven
Did I make a wish,
And God made you come to be.

The miracle of love
Is an instance of eternity.

Do You Remember

*N*estled in the caverns of my memories is the
vision that can simply be described only as you.
Gaze upon the twinkle, in the light of my eyes, as a
reflection of our journey through this passageway to
infinity called life. Each moment shared is engraved on the
memoirs of my heart. Each communion is a celebration of
our storied embrace. Can you see the silhouette of
our shadows in the night? Do you recall true love's first
kiss? Did you know, at that moment, two lovers'
heartbeats, they would never care to miss?
Mmm . . . so did I.

The melody of love
Is an orchestra of imagination.

Calypso Across My Heart

The rhythm that moves in me is played by the orchestra of your advances. The words on the lyric sheet explode into dance upon the entrance to your celestial stage.
I hear the bells chime as every move you make is a symphony only matched by the pen of Mozart. With every step you take towards me, with every finger you trace behind my ear, oh how it creates, such a passionate serenade. More than a waltz, an interlude of romance, a calypso across my heart.

II

A Poetic Look At Life

My Process of Thoughts

*T*his montage of existence we call life is a beautiful thing. It is a roller coaster of challenges and emotions. It is family, it is friends. It is looking back on memories, it is reflecting on the ones we've lost, and how we view ourselves in the universe. It is a voyage where we search to know who we are. It is the appreciation of the peacefulness of home. Though often arduous in scope we should be thankful for each day we rise and are able to behold the warmth of the sun's glow. *A Poetic Look At Life* says in words what we see daily and how we live out the script of our lives.

A kinship that lasts and never ends,
Is the bond between true friends.

Friends

Never lovers, yet always friends,
Who knew two wondering hearts,
Would together travel a road,
That unreservedly never ends.

No one knows our struggles,
The walls and barriers we had to take down,
But we lifted each other up,
So that our feet below
Would not traverse the broken glass,
That covered a shaky ground.

You were there in the beginning,
You helped me to start,
The love of your name,
Is engraved on my heart.

This is for all the valleys,
That we've both walked through,
For the tears that turned to joy and how you
remained true.
For every success I've had and all that I do,
I will always cherish our friendship,
And celebrate what I have with you.

Treasure the one who gave you birth
For no greater love exists in all the earth.

Ode To My Mother

*F*or all that you endured, taught me and shared,
You asked for nothing, and nothing was spared.
You gave all that you had.
With wounded body you toiled to make fresh bread,
So that our bodies would be nourished as you
laid us down in bed.

Unfailing love is all that I knew from you,
Ten thousand lives could I live,
And not know how you could take so little,
And do what you would do.
I would not be able to pay you back for all that you've given,
Blessed we were all the days that you were living.

I love you Mother, I miss you so much,
Not just dinner on Sundays,
But your warm and gentle touch.
That place in my heart, left by you remains vacant,
Because there is no love born of mortal men,
That could be deemed a replacement.

I live on because of you and hope I've made you proud,
I wish you could see in person what
your sons have become,
You would rejoice, I know, out loud.
Missing you every day and wanting to hear,
"you know what you have to do,"
Those were all the words I needed
To help me face anything,

I was going through.
Keep moving forward you said,
Be myself, no one else will do,
To be the best I can,
You taught me that too.

Hold fast the prayers, I send each and every night,
For with all my love and thankfulness,
They do take flight.

Allow me to be me
And we both will be free.

Gotta Be Me

You cannot change me,
for I can only be who I am.
My flaws, my good, all my bad,
What makes me happy, what makes me sad.
My size, my color, the texture of my skin,
The fullness of my lips, how my words begin.
If the person you have come to know,
Is not the one whose time you seek,
The open door of life,
Has others for you to meet.

We must take back our sons,
From the flawed scene of ignorance and guns.

Generation Lost

*T*here is a subject we all must start to talk about,
We need everyone to listen, even those with clout.
We have to reach and grab, those twenty and under,
Save them from gangs and streets full of reckless plunder.

There was nothing called time out for you and for me,
We got beat with whatever was close,
I think I was introduced to the trunk of a tree.
Young people must have discipline, they must
learn respect,
The more we lose to violence and feelings of hopelessness,
The more of our future we will regret.

How can the doctors and experts
Tell us how to raise our young,
Who gave our children the right to defy us,
And then dial 911.

We got beat up where we cut up, no falling
down in supermarket aisles,
My mother, the relatives and the neighbors,
Never worried a whipping would send them to trial.

The boys have no dreams, the girls with skirts
two inches high,
Whatever they see on TV, they go outside and try.
We have to get their attention, our chant has to say,
"Free their minds from the prison,
Of not finding a better way."

They have to know just hanging out and playing
video games isn't all there is,
Pants hanging on their ankles, when they get
old how will they live?
I have two sons and four nephews, I'm gonna do all I can,
To show them thug life is short-lived,
And there's so much more to being a man.

Evolution involves you.

Change

*I*f I go, you must let me leave.
If it's time, then leave you must,
No drama of rage and regret of going,
A simple case of diminished trust.

Let me go, and I too must set you free,
Those tiny movements on the face of our clock,
Have all run its course,
alarm gone off, for you and me.

What I grew to love about you will always remain the same,
We must accept that the world turns on a mysterious axis,
With only one constant,

Change.

My search is over.

Take Me

*F*rom the border of tranquility have I toiled to
make known my intentions. In the blink of an eye
have I determined my destination.
Sent by spirits of longing, who also planted
my inspiration. Anchored in love, do I offer my
charred hands, in hope you would
accept me, as yours.

With every new day you see, rejoice.

Happy

Awakened by the sound of drum patterns in the rain,
My heart opens up, to a new passion to sing.
Running and jumping flying in the air,
My mind sails on a vision of spirit, a will of no care.

I long for the day, I chase the night,
Living is a privilege of which I do not take light.
I smell the roses, I picnic in the grass of green,
Filled with enlightenment, on a kite of
yellow moon beams.

Joy, oh joy, this moment of mine,
I see beyond valleys of mystery and surf on pillars of dimes.
And when the clear hourglass has released,
Its last morsel of diamond crystal sand,
I rejoice in my slumber, for the morning holds for me,
The chance to live, over and over again.

Embrace the wind.

The Wind Blows Through

I cannot see you, yet I feel you there,
You run lines across my body as an artist,
Whose canvas with free spirit,
begs him and brush to dare.

What is your origin how does your current flow?
From the north, south, east, and west do your travels blow.
I love you in winter, when the cool of your caress,
Chills the hollow places in my mind,
creating blissful zest.

Devoid of physical touch, yet you hold fast
your powerful way,
Your force crumbles objects of brick and mortar,
Still how I cherish you making me sway.

And what of the warmth you bring,
That changes the course, of a jagged stream.
Where did you come from, how did you come to be?
Never mind the answer, just consume my
senses on the ocean's shore,
And blow through me.

What do you see
When you look upon this place called earth?

Through My Eyes

*O*n ice covered peaks I sit, looking at the
mountains in the distance,
How magnificent the site,
The grandeur of their existence.

I look upon the ocean,
And the deep blue sea,
And I realize,
I am but a pebble in the sand,
An atom of eternity.

I feel the air that only a blind man can see,
Yet I know it binds my spirit and all its majesty.
And what of the sun, the stars, the moon,
The glow that brings light and warmth,
To the roses in spring, that come to bloom.

Who am I to say how all these things began,
For born of life by a whisper,
Was the birth of man.

He who adjusts to the twists and turns
of the roads less traveled,
Finds the path to strength
In the lanes of the straight and narrow.

The River Bends

*F*or miles the journey reaches,
As the earth gives way to its command,
Nothing will thwart its ending settlement,
Not even the malice of man.

Trees let go their tangled grip,
Of the deep grounded soil,
It is a part of the voyage, to struggle and toil.
Onward must it travel,
To the place of its genesis,
Facing difficult turns,
often called its nemesis.

Without care of what looms ahead,
Through twists and turns and savage terrain,
Its mission intact, for nothing
its course will change.

It travels home to meet the waves,
Where its beginning remains,
Such is the walk of life,
does it not do the same?

Laughter warms the heart and tickles the soul.

Smile

Such a simple gesture, a feeling of youth,
How wondrous the sensation,
To know someone is smiling at you.

Smile, through the pitfalls and plagues of life,
The moment you show that pleasantry,
One knows everything is alright.

Smile at the shimmer of the sweet morning dew,
For when you smile at others,
Your light moves all it covers,
And your inner beauty comes
roaring through.

Cherish Always The Celebrated Lives

Shirley Marie Lynch
Yul LaMorton Lynch
David "Top" Lynch
Billy Ray Lynch
Frederick Banard Lynch Jr.
Fairyn Lynch
J-Nabia DaSha Johnson
Patsy Ann Johnson
Matilda & Algie Dickson
Rev. A. Simmons
Sis. Effie Green
Mr. Nelson L. Evans
Mr. Claude McCain Jr.
Mr. J. L. Killings
Mrs. Mary McGinnis
Mr. Wendall W. James
Mrs. Gladys Hunt
Mr. A. T. DeVaughn
Mr. Herman DeVaughn Sr.
Uncle Walter Coleman
Mary "Aunt Heavy" Coleman
Mr. Alfred Jones Jr.
Mrs Katherine Louise Johnson
Mrs. Ruby Nell Strawther
Coach Sam West
Alan Ray Hall

For Those Who've Gone Home

*E*very night I pray,
I'm thankful for the day,
I was blessed by your love,
Even though you've gone away.

How much do I remember,
The hearts you gave,
So warm and tender.
So many have we lost,
So many I cannot say,
How we all miss you so,
Because you've gone away.

We toil and we tarry,
Through days that get hairy,
We struggle and we plead,
For understanding of our deeds.
Knowing to the core, we'll again see your face,
Travel on streets of gold,
In that most hallowed place.

So today we pay homage to you,
For all those gone ahead, who helped us make it through.
To the days and nights that seem so long,
We will always miss, love and remember,
Those who've gone home.

Love them or leave them, Your family is yours.

Family

I shall always remember the holidays, at Grandma's house,
It would always be entertaining, of that you could have no doubt.
We would tease and joke so much, we always had fun,
We ate and played dominoes until the day was done.

My mother was Shirley, she was the best cook,
If you tried one of those mystery dishes from my aunts,
That was just a chance you took.

I remember my favorite aunt, bless her heart, made some stew,
No one could bear the taste but didn't know what to do.
So we slipped it out back and fed the dogs through that old fence,
That was the last meal we served them, they ran away,
ain't seen them since.

There were always great stories,
Too many to remember to tell,
But there was always that uncle or cousin,
Who just got out of jail.

And then there were those with the paper bags,
And those who had to slip away back to the tree,
Everyone knew what they were doing,
The smell would set you free.

There was always a new baby, didn't know where
they came from sometimes,
But if you waited, you would find out,
An aunt would pick them up and tell it all,

She didn't move too fast, she had a little
sugar and a little gout.

Proud the parents were, new blood to carry the name,
To the first-time visitors, we acted up so much,
They thought us all strange.

No matter our differences,
even when we fussed or would fight,
The elders reminded us we were kin,
we better make it right.
At the end of the day, there were lots of hugs,
No matter our struggles, we always shared love.

There is nothing like family,
even the one you gave money,
And you knew you weren't getting it back,
What is it about friends and kinfolk,
That makes them act like that.

Yes there is nothing like family,
just like there is no place like home,
What a wonderful thing to know you
have people who love you,
A place to lay your head in times of need,
All the day long.

Lift up your head, believe with all your essence that you can be what you choose. Choose wisely.

To A Young Man

*W*here are you going, do you even know?
Are you lead by your loins, are you ready to grow?
So much awaits you, so much for you to see,
But your world is filled with a chant me me me.

Where you come from may matter,
But only if it's an excuse to fall back,
To take your eyes away from the prize,
Only throws you off track.

There's more to this world,
Than how much you can spread your seed,
Getting high on "pharmaceutical extractions"
wine and weed.
For some I have no worry, for some I have no fear,
It's the ones who've lost respect for life and all others,
Humanity they no longer hold dear.

In the streets and in the 'hood,
Why have you become so bad, so up to no good?
Is it lack of hope, no father or jobs to be found?
There has to be a better way,
To keep you out of jail, or putting you in the ground.

I applaud many of you, who choose education and stand,
For a belief that character,
not violence is the true measure of a man.
So to all choose life, your community,
your dreams, and never stay blue,

I rose from the coldness of linoleum floors and you can to.
To do wrong is easy, to always do right
is the hardest thing to do,
Don't let those headlines say, "*Died too young*,"
don't let that be you.

Though heavy your burdens,
Fear not,
For I will help bring light to your load.

Young Mother

*E*very day is a struggle
Yet you do the best you can,
No help from the state
No support from a man.

Torn shoes but clean clothes do you lay,
Before they're off to school,
Before they're out to play.

You're too young a mother,
Not old enough to have a child,
Where have we gone as a people,
When babies having babies are in style.

I see the pain of your efforts,
I see the tears on your face,
I wish I had more to give,
Than food for you to taste.

Somehow you have to keep trying,
For your children you have to go on,
Life rarely forgives many of those,
Who too soon wanted to be grown.

I see you at the bus stop,
doing what you have to do,
Because it's right and I know you're trying,
I will help you through.
And when the load gets too heavy,

and you just have to rest,
I will lift you up because I know
you're doing your very best.

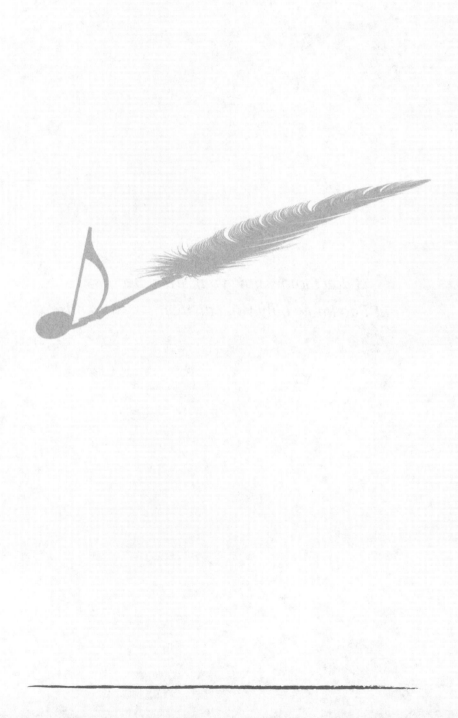

I don't know how your story began,
But I do know only you can write how it ends.

To The Pan Man

*W*ho was the fool
That thought it cool
To bail on knowledge, drop out of school
To live on ignorance and breaking the rules,
No plans for life, just living crude.

So sad it is, so sad is this,
You go through changes and all the twists.
Just to find
A bottle of wine
To beg on streets,
For a dollar or a dime.

What must it take
For you to see,
You must have something
Which you believe,
Something in life you can achieve.
To beg and plead was not your plan,
To steal a meal from a helping hand.

Not your fault, maybe it was,
To live in shame, not in love.
I don't know your story,
I don't know your plight,
I see what's wrong,
Only you can make it right.

You must have the will
To say until,
Life is over
You want to live.

You must have hope
You have to try,
Or stand on the corner,
And wonder why.

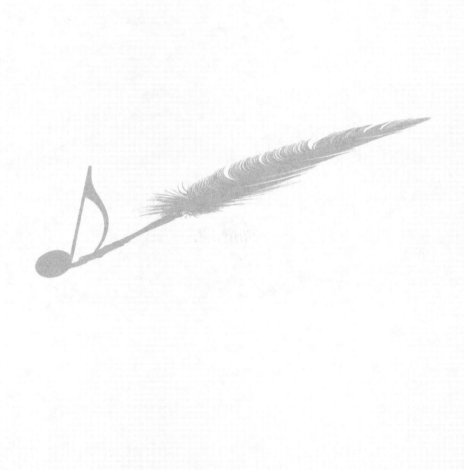

Finish it!

The Last Corner

*Y*ou just couldn't do it,
You couldn't take the last drop,
Of Mom's special Kool-Aid
Even on a summer day too hot.

Why can't we just finish the pitcher,
And stop leaving a little sip or a corner,
Just like when you did the dishes and left the pots,
It was just something, something you didn't wanna.

It didn't have to be the special lemonade,
It could be just water, tea or milk,
What is it about that last swallow,
That leaves you with such guilt?

I don't know what to tell you,
I've done it myself.
Why did I put the bottle back in the refrigerator,
When only a corner was left.

Elation is the doorway to celebration.

It's On

*R*un, run, it's time for fun,
Just got paid, my day is done.
Worked all week, gave it all I could,
I hope I made a difference
Always thought I would.

Run, run, it's time for fun
Lets get the party started
For two whole days I'm done.
Friday is my night, to let my hair down,
Gonna go bust a move,
Like there was no one else around.

Out of my way, I'm headed for the door,
Step to the side quick or you'll be knocked to the floor.
The weekend has come, so much to do and see,
I hope the city has its gloves on,
I hope they're ready for me.

Take me back down memory lane,
So that I may toast those jewels again.

Old School

Remember when Mom went to work
And it was just your sister, brother and you,
The world opened to many possibilities,
Of deviltry for you to do.

I couldn't wait to get outside,
Because if she was home,
That street light,
Better not catch you out,
If darkness fell too soon to get inside,
That was a twelve-round bout.

What about that government cheese?
Why was that sandwich so good?
Add some fried bologna,
you smelt it all through the neighborhood.

I use to always get in trouble,
When we played "hide and go get it,"
Why did I always end up with the girls,
Who were ready to come with it.

We use to fight if you were from another street,
Your best buddy was one who had your back,
We were crazy and mannish,
after watching "Dudley Do-Right"
We tied poor little Jackie Collins to a railroad track.

There was always some fool,
who thought sniffing paint was cool.
Man, I wish I had just one day back at my
senior year in high school.
The stories I could tell,
would make your head bust and swell,
Man, I miss dancing to that old hit,
You Can Ring My Bell.

To hear you is to see you
To touch you is to know you.

Back In The Day

*W*e used to play back in the day,
We laughed and joked at each other's ways,
There was no box of silicon and glass to hide behind,
We shared our thoughts, it gave us peace of mind.

It's not the same when you talk from another place,
How do I really know what your saying,
when I can't see your face.
But what did we do when we didn't have cell phones,
And now spend millions on some ring or
finding the perfect tone.

Back in the day we learned relationships needed nurturing,
If they were going to be,
Now when you meet someone for the first time,
It's no telling what you may see.

Some of the pics you get are thirty years old,
And you don't even know then if it was real or sold.
I know we live in different times,
Change comes to bring an easier way,
But if you really want to know someone,
Invest your time in the person,
like we did back in the day.

The music of nature is in every praise of wonderment.

Bird Of Song

*F*rom the window in my room,
I see you nestled in the tree.
Perched on a woven nest,
You start your morning song.

Sprinkled leaves of orange and gold,
Are the back drop of your platform
There, in a moment of infinity,
I see you seeing me and your notes take flight.

The clouds drifted in to disappearance.
The rainbow skies adorned the day.
Who knew the sound of one so fair, seen so rare,
Would bring calm to the early morning air.

A swallow you are called by name,
A musician of nature whose gift is to sing.
With so much in the world so crazy and so much wrong,
I find peace in the melody of your expression,
I delight in your morning song.

Be it ever so humble . . .

Home

*I*t is the end of the day
And no how no way,
There's a thing you can do,
To make me stay.
To my place of refuge must I go,
Where I may lay my head and
let tranquil thought flow.

It is in my place, it is in my domain
That I feel at ease, nowhere else is the same.
Barefoot or bare skinned
When I close the door
No one has to come in.
Home is where I find peace
Through sunshine or rain,
It is my castle,
Nowhere else is the same.

Smooth is the gray-haired dude
Who still lives his life cool.

Cat Daddy Rap

*H*ey pretty lady, so you wanna know what you are to me?
Cool, then sit down and let me break it down to you like this,
Let me see . . .
You're the cream in my coffee
The tootsie in my roll
You set fire to my senses
Your smile burns my soul
You're the honey on my bun
You're the green in my tea
I bless the earth you walk on
I can hardly contain you wanting to be with me
You're the butter on my biscuit
You're the grape in my wine
I thank the sun, the moon, and the stars
You are truly one-of-a-kind

More you say?

You're the stars in my sky
Your love makes me high
You're the wood in my fire
You fill me with desire
You know I'm not a liar
Now let's go home
So I can take you higher.

Now give me some sugar.

The lines on my face are the pathways
that lead me to the now.

The Mirror Talks

When you look in the mirror
Tell me what do you see
Who is that person staring back at me?
Do I know you? Are you for real?
Where are you going with time to kill?

What do you see with eyes looking at me?
Where will you go when your mind doesn't know?
How can you stand, stand there and stare?
Who are you to look at me and care with such a glare?

Do you have a name, are you really me?
My friend out there, what do you see?
When you look in the mirror, is it really you,
Or is it a filler of broken glass,
Trying to pretend it knows what to do?

I know not my own lines that cross my aged face,
But only you can show me evidence of its
ruff and withered date.
Though you are not real, a living breathing thing,
Is it me I see, or an illusion or a dream?

Tease me not.

Shadows In The Mist

*Y*es, yes, there you are
And again you come to me
In the twilight of the night.
Are you real?
What allows you to cross waves of water?
Who are those you emulate
As I sit before you
And you so eloquently entertain me?
From the color of the hour,
Has time lost its power,
And in stillness here I sit in the wonderment.
So serene it seems in your mystic gleam,
Am I drawn by your silent suggestions.
Yes, yes, now I see,
Formed is your shape
Of transparency.
Come to me no more
Old mirage of tangles and twists,
Temptation without satisfaction are you,
These shadows in the mist.

III

Inspired Thoughts

My Process of Thoughts

I believe there are people who exist that were born to do great things. This was their calling, it is their purpose. They overcome their maladies and never accept anything less than what they desire. They look in the mirror and tell themselves daily they decide their own fate. In their spirit is a belief that there is nothing they cannot do. Many adhere to the idea that their mission was of divine design. Others find peace in the mere knowledge that they stand for something bigger than themselves and their legacy is not about what they did for self but what was done in the service of others. Time equates to an opportunity to enhance their lives rather than pity themselves for the conditions of their environment. Some will have trials so difficult few will be able to comprehend. I am a long way from where I came from and still farther yet from where I plan to be. *Inspired Thoughts* comes from a place of intimate knowledge of life's struggles and the perseverance and persistence one needs to live life victoriously.

With each mind and spirit you enrich,
The greater the harvest of inspired souls.

Relevance

*R*un when there is no race
Push when you can no longer pull
Fight to make it right
Run in Spain with the bulls.
Leap when you're afraid to jump
Try when you don't think you can
If you don't win the race
Make them know you ran.
And when you win, always remain humble,
Let no one make your dreams crumble.
Give when there's no time for giving,
Light a fire of hope for the unforgiving,
In all that struggle with the lives they're living.
Dance on the sun, sail on the moon
Pick up the torch for all of those
Who made their mark, but left us too soon.
Make sure you let the world know,
After you're gone, you left evidence you were here,
You dared to do the impossible,
Opened blinded eyes of nothingness,
And cured the oppression of fear.
You charged through the storms
You made cloudy minds all the more clear,
Left your mark on the world,
And for you they gave cheer.

No matter the circumstance,
You determine your resolution of change.

I Made It Out

*F*rom the cold brick walls I came,
Never knowing what it was to have a legal last name.
Plastic floors and addresses connected,
The color of my skin, in searching for work,
a reason to be rejected.
Thin walls that made the gossip so clear,
How can there be privacy when the voices are so near?
One pinch with a pin through those paper-thin walls,
And no family could hide a secret,
the streets knew them all.
So many died before me,
so many died as my contemporaries,
Those that had a future,
and those destined for early obituaries.
Each day was a fight,
people pushed not to lose their minds,
When you live in the ghetto you have a life of free time.
It's funny, in those days,
we didn't know we were poor,
We always had enough,
never knowing if we needed more.
My mother worked three jobs
and we lived for Christmas day,
It was a moment of real happiness that helped her
three boys not to stray.
A girl nine-years-old had a baby
some felt it was fine,
Sex is a part of recreation in the 'hood,
it helps fill the time.

Now here I stand, removed from the
place, that molded the man.
Grateful for the day,
I got to see beyond the concrete walls,
Whoever knew green grass grew,
beyond those playground halls.

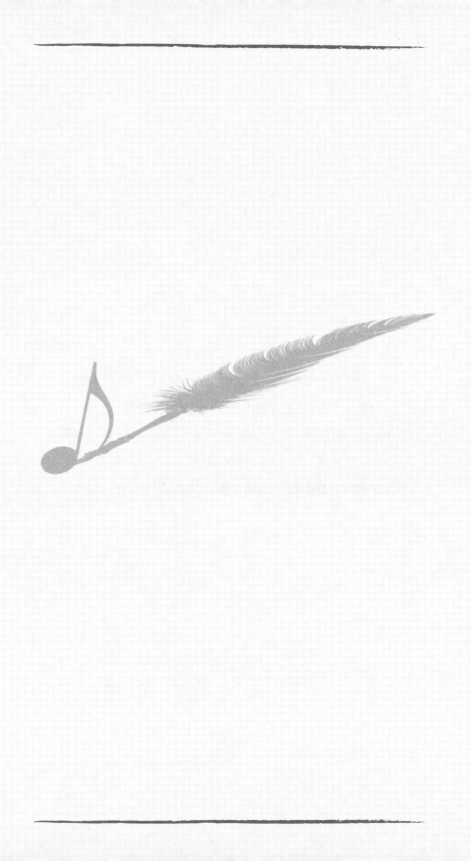

*In the footnote of your malevolence is the
encryption of your audience,
Whose signature is the grace of your love, peace
everlasting.
Serenity waits on the other side of decision.*

A Love For All Seasons

*I*t is written, there is a time and place
For everything. A season for all
Beneath the heavens.

I have seen this place in the sky,
I have looked upon eternal joy,
And found that the kingdom of providence,
Lives within each of us, it is a plan not a ploy.
The door of light that stands closed, beckons you,
To turn the 'knob and take the first step,
It is called free will, it is a part of your prep.

The serenity that awaits,
Will not stop a cold world from turning on you,
Or keep dark clouds at bay,
But it shall give you peace,
In the epicenter of the storm,
Belief in knowing that soon comes a brighter day.
A security in the knowledge that will always last,
Seeing the beauty of the rainbow's arrival,
Will surely come to pass.

Turn on your will.

Flip The Switch

*I*n darkness do I dwell,
Here in this hollow place,
Reaching out to nothingness,
That I might feel the lines on my face.

In this hour of solitude,
Lost in this condemned cave,
Locked in noise with no one to save.

I look in a mirror, that I cannot see,
I fear its reflection, for the monster is me.
Then the sound of thunder, roared a loud shrieking tone,
Finally I achieved repentance,
I turned on the light,
And was no longer alone.

The sure cure for procrastination,
Is to do it now. Press on.

Presistence

*D*on't wait, do it now someway, somehow.
Stop talking about all your dreams,
And all you know you can be,
There's no excuse now, results count,
Something tangible I can see.

I don't want to hear that problems,
Too often hold you back,
there's a Black Man in the White House,
Not in our lifetime, did we ever think we'd see that?

Take your passion, take your trade, create your own path,
for you it was made.
Race always to win; yes, you will stumble,
You may start humbly but never give up, never crumble.

Never stop believing, know there's an expected end,
To a prize of promise, broken hearts will mend.
Talent alone is not enough,
when days are long, hard, and tough.
Your pursuit must be constant,
Never yielding to resistance,
For to achieve a dream, you must be relentless,
Driven by the vehicle,
Called endless persistence.

The conception of thought, triggers the ignition of choice,
The direction you take, solidifies the consequence of that decision.

Choice

*T*he mirror of my mind reflects not what I see as I stand
in the presence of images. More than any misconception,
it only represents the me for that moment. A snapshot of
my predilections or the errands of life I must run before
the sun's hour of rest. I must take what I see, assure my
thoughts it is me, control my chances to be, what the
reflection has chosen to conceive.

To all: Answer your call.

We Need You

*C*rackled and crumbled does the world flow,
Layered in dust do you stand from head to toe.
Torn of the struggle to find your place in worth,
To bring some justification of existence,
Before they cover you with dirt.

If you become a father you must be a man,
To save our sons and daughters we must,
Before they fall in the perils of life,
A cruel and dirty quicksand.

Educate their minds,
you scream we must do,
Our time, talent and guidance,
Is what will help them get through.

If you have made it,
don't get lost with self,
Go back and pull at least one,
Who so many times, have no one else.
Money alone is not enough,
there's so much work,
and so little trust.

Live to make a difference
before you fall in that forever sleep,
And those that crowd your resting place,
Try to find a reason to weep.

To our people all around the world,
We must pull together and alert,
Do what you can to save a race,
Before they cover you in dirt.

If you watch the sands of the hourglass dissipate,
The empty space is what you didn't do.

Time

*S*o often do we take for granted
This cycle of existence called time.
For it is more than simply a measure of seconds,
Passing through a state of entropy in one's own mind.
Moreover, it is an opportunity,
That cascades from the genesis of thought,
Holding a plethora of options,
To be what we will.

I will not forsake my favor.

I Believe

*T*orn by uncertainty, blinded by doubt
I believe
Knocked down, scolded, and held back
I still believe
Arrows that stare in my face
Yet, I press on
Because I believe
Pulled from side-to-side, doors closed
Even as I stand alone,
Again I believe.
Knocked down and cast adrift,
With no help and crocodiles chomping at my knees,
Yes, I still do believe.
Why?

"I can do all things through . . ."

If you give up, you won't get done.

Turn Away Dark Clouds

*T*urn away dark clouds,
I have no time for you now.
You come only to bring me down.
I won't let you take me there,
So be gone, I don't need you around.

I've seen you push many to the brink and the break,
You made going on a 50/50 proposition,
but it's an offer I couldn't take.
I have to keep pushing on,
I will fight to make it right,
I will not let your trouble days keep me from the light.

Turn away dark clouds,
I have to keep marching ahead,
Your doubt and self pity will not be my yokes,
I'm strong enough now to keep you out of my head.

I've made it through your storms,
I've endured the rain,
I've replaced loss of hope with determination,
where there once was pain.
You should have had me when I fell
and moved in for the kill,
But you're too late now, for I live in favor,
in His perfect will.
I lifted myself up from the depths of a troubled life,
I've stared at the inside of my soul
and overcame my strife.

So turn away dark clouds go run, go hide,
You no longer have a hold on me,
here you no longer abide.
Turn away dark clouds, turn away and run,
From the moment I found real joy,
My strength flourished, my life began anew, yes,
it has truly begun.

Your gift is your lift.

Purpose Divine

*O*ver hills and mountains have I climbed,
A bitter search to find meaning,
A purpose divine.

But what is purpose divine?
Why do the roots of an oak dive so deep?
Why does the moon hold on course the earth,
How do the day and nighttime meet?

What is it that you have, what talent is true?
For it is that blessing, that is unique to you.
Into the world it must be released,
Its power revealed, will call storms to cease.
This is divine purpose—*the exaltation of your gift,*
For many in humanity await your calling,
Magnified in reason,
their spirits you will lift.

Now that I'm at the mountain's peak,
I must live to be higher.

I've Arrived

*E*very morning when I wake
I know I'm blessed for goodness sake
The day is mine for me to make
Only I can walk through that gate
Of broken dreams of love and hate
The meter is running, drive is my rate.
So much to do, so much at stake,
No time for honey, little time for cake.
When I reach the top I will not forsake,
Loved ones who envisioned I could be great.
I will look back on the memories and start a new slate,
Thankful for the man, the Master did create.

In all you do
Find your place of tranquility.

Strawberry Fields

*I*n to the fields I travel tasting the sweetness of the air.
The sun which brings life to all, warms me and gives moisture to
my face. The rolling hills are a picturesque frame
to a landscape to what must describe heaven on canvas.
For as far as the eyes can see, meadows are filled with
strawberry hills. I stop to take in the wonderment,
and the pleasure of the berries' aroma lifts me to flight.
All is in harmony, as only music covers the crystal blue springs.
Let me lose my heart here in this place, let me release my mind,
in these strawberry fields.

The world cannot know peace,
Until there is calm in its chaos.

I Dream Of A Day

I dream of a day when the world
Will open its arms, to men of all nations,
People of all colors, beings of all genders.

I dream of a day when hate has found
Its way to a forgotten thought,
That we all respect the existence,
Of our right to our own space in this universe.

I dream of a day when hunger
Is but a case study for a class, history in a glass.
I dream of humanity realizing that
beneath the heavens we are one species,
The human race, we share the air, we care for our earth.

I dream of a day when fear, has no place
In how we live,
And respect
Has removed the screams of prejudice.
I dream of a time when the life of one less fortunate,
Is as equal of those of noble birth.
Not from a place of wealth, shall one be measured,
But as one who deserves
The right to voice why they are relevant.

I dream of a day of peace,
A time when you could open a window
And enjoy the air without the thought of a
stranger invading your moment.

I dream of a day when we all say we are one,
We stand united against all matters
of oppression and aggression.
I dream of a day.
I dream of that day.

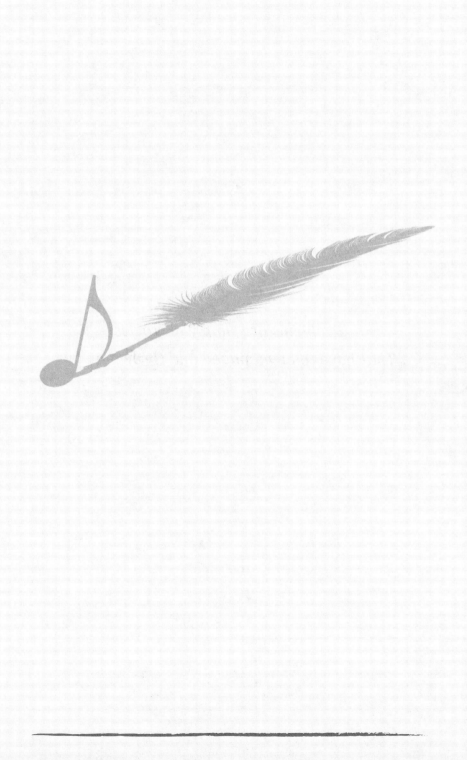

Problems are simply obstacles
That have to be managed and thrown away.

A Pebble In My Shoe

I know there's something, something I've just got to do,
I've got to get rid of this pebble,
This pebble in my shoe.

For years it has haunted me,
For years it has caused me pain,
With every day that passes,
I didn't fulfill my promise,
In its place the pebble remained.

I've got to get going,
I've got to do what I need to do,
That's the only way I'm going to get this pebble,
This pebble from my shoe.

Every moment I put it off,
The grief grows more and more.
The very best waits,
On the other side of that door.

Yes, that's it,
I have to finish what I start,
I must light a fire under my will,
I need a new mark.
Stop talking about what I'm going to do,
And just do what I'm talking about,
That's the only way I'm going to throw this pebble,
Throw this pebble out.

Be strong all of you that are young,
Prepare yourselves, for the beauty and trials
of life to come.

There There Little Man

*T*here, there, little man,
Why do you cry over castles of sand?
Do you not know,
That all in time must wither and flow?

Weep not for the pebbles that drift away,
Know that your youth alone,
gives chance to another day.
Take the dirt, in to the palms of your hands,
Fashion it like clay as I know you can.

Bring to life what has sailed away to sea,
It is your time to grow and no time to flee.
Lift up your head always, face the sky,
Stress not the little things,
for those never cry.

So there now little man,
What is it you see, in washed-away sand?
A chance to rebuild again and again
rests with you in the palm of your hand.
An opportunity to create from nothing,
a host of realized dreams,
To share your light with the world,
via inspiring shining springs.

Dare now little man,
Mold your future, like I know you can.
You were born for greatness;

you are destined to lead,
And to inspire the hearts of men,
your mantra is to succeed.

My mind is at rest on the shores of the water's edge.

Mellow Waters

*R*eclining and relaxed I sit in the aura of your movement. Your waves shimmer as the moon colors you with diamonds and emeralds. I stand, as a gesture to take in more of your elixir of softness, and the rhythm of your grooves, as your refreshing chill clinches my feet. Lost in consciousness I am subdued by the munificent way you allow me to collect and explore my visions. I'm at rest in your sequence. I am at peace in your vastness. Carry my thoughts to oblivion sweet waters of mellow moods.

Free is the heart that gives
So that others may live.

For Those Who Choose Life

*M*ay you always see the light,
To help you find your way,
May you never know the hunger of a
hopeless, darkened day.

And when the clouds arrive
I pray you strength
And the will to survive.
And when the storm has passed,
I wish the joy would always last.

May you face the winter cold
knowing there soon comes the spring,
May you see beauty in most all that exists,
Even the common and very little things.

And when the world has you cornered,
And your back is up against the wall,
Fight to forge ahead,
You may stumble, but don't you ever fall.

May you always see life,
As a chance to grow and give,
So when it's time for blissful rest,
We shall celebrate how you lived.

About The Author

E. Arabis Zemill began writing many years ago and is now putting those thoughts into published form. Born and residing in Dallas, Texas, he has traveled extensively to a myriad of places and confesses that, to him, vacation means time on white sand shores. A high school multi-sport athlete who lettered in football, basketball, and track, he went on to receive a scholarship to play football at Southern Methodist University. He had aspirations of a pro career but life chose for him a different path. He decided to go to work for the largest transportation company in the world, where he is currently an operations manager. After several promotions, he returned to Southern Methodist University and acquired a degree in Economics. A well-rounded renaissance man, and now author, he is also a singer and songwriter. He has three more books in the pipeline, including one which speaks to the real dynamics of the relationships between men and women. Also on the horizon are three movie scripts, a line of t-shirts, and his own lyrical publishing company. He is truly a man on a mission.

"Prose is edgy and fresh with great visualization that pulls you in and holds you. I am really looking forward to his future work and know that he has great things in store for his readers!"

—Dr. Veurmer Clark
Optometrist

"E. Arabis Zemill has successfully combined the writers pen with the musical note. His ability to express beautiful thoughts is amazing."

—David A. Small
Entertainment Attorney

"I kept finding myself saying Wow. Not only is E. Arabis Zemill a truly gifted writer, but he touches every emotion and his words are extremely relevant in many aspects of life."

—Jama Drake
VP of Sales Impelsys Inc.